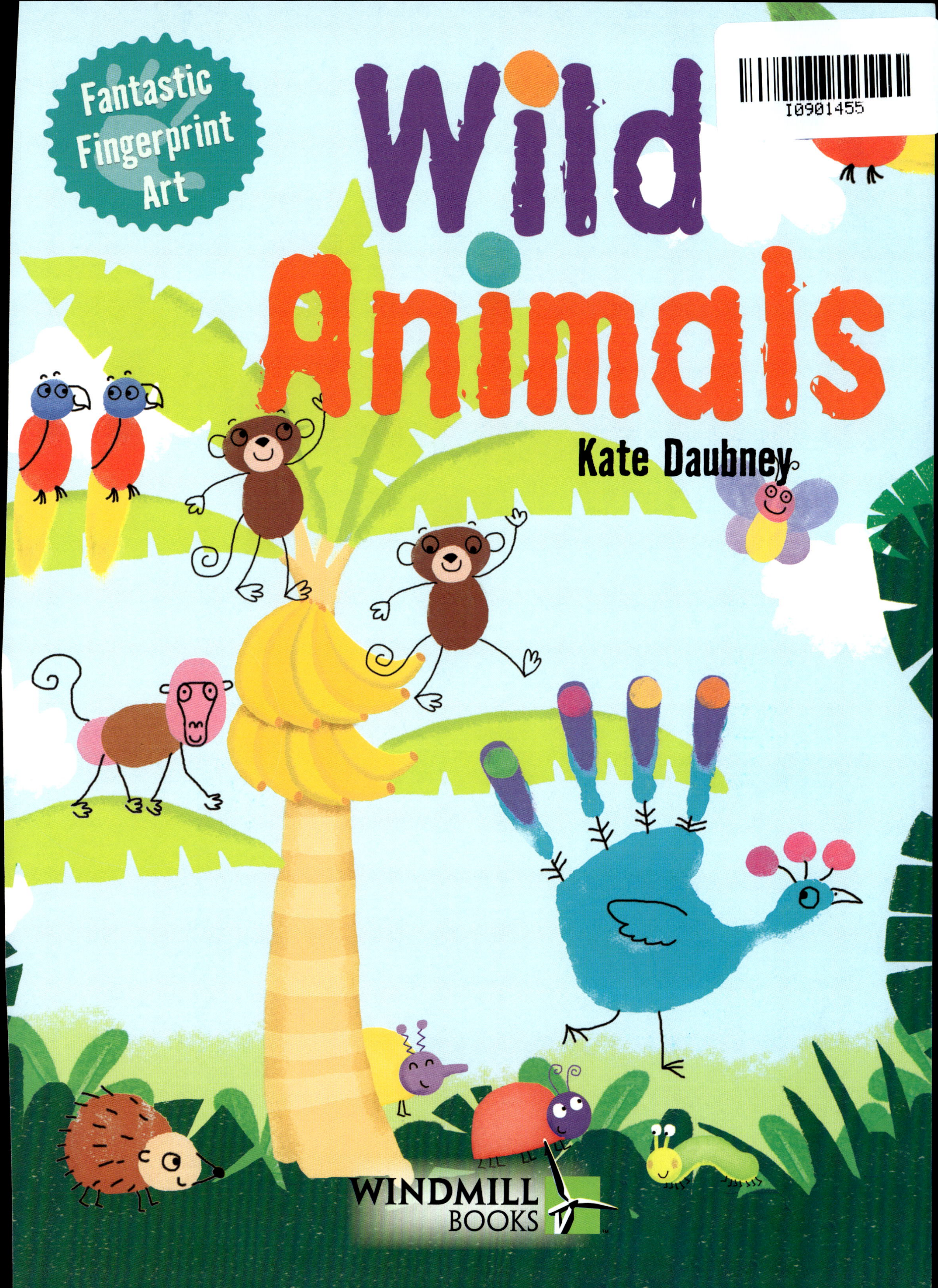
Fantastic Fingerprint Art
Wild Animals
Kate Daubney
WINDMILL BOOKS

Published in 2019 by Windmill Books,
an Imprint of Rosen Publishing
29 East 21st Street, New York, NY 10010

Illustrated by Kate Daubney
Written and edited by Susannah Bailey
Designed by Square and Circus with Emma Randall

Cataloging-in-Publication Data

Names: Daubney, Kate.
Title: Wild animals / Kate Daubney.
Description: New York : Windmill Books, 2019. | Series: Fantastic fingerprint art
Identifiers: LCCN ISBN 9781508195351 (pbk.) | ISBN 9781508195344 (library bound) | ISBN 9781508195368 (6 pack)
Subjects: LCSH: Fingerprints in art--Juvenile literature. | Animals in art--Juvenile literature. | Drawing--Technique--Juvenile literature.
Classification: LCC NC825.F55 D38 2019 | DDC 743.6--dc23

Manufactured in the United States of America

CPSIA Compliance Information: Batch BS18WM:
For Further Information contact Rosen Publishing, New York, New York at 1-800-237-9932

FINGERPRINTING IS FUN!

In this book you'll learn how to paint your very own fingerprint animals. To do this, you'll need to use different parts of your fingers.

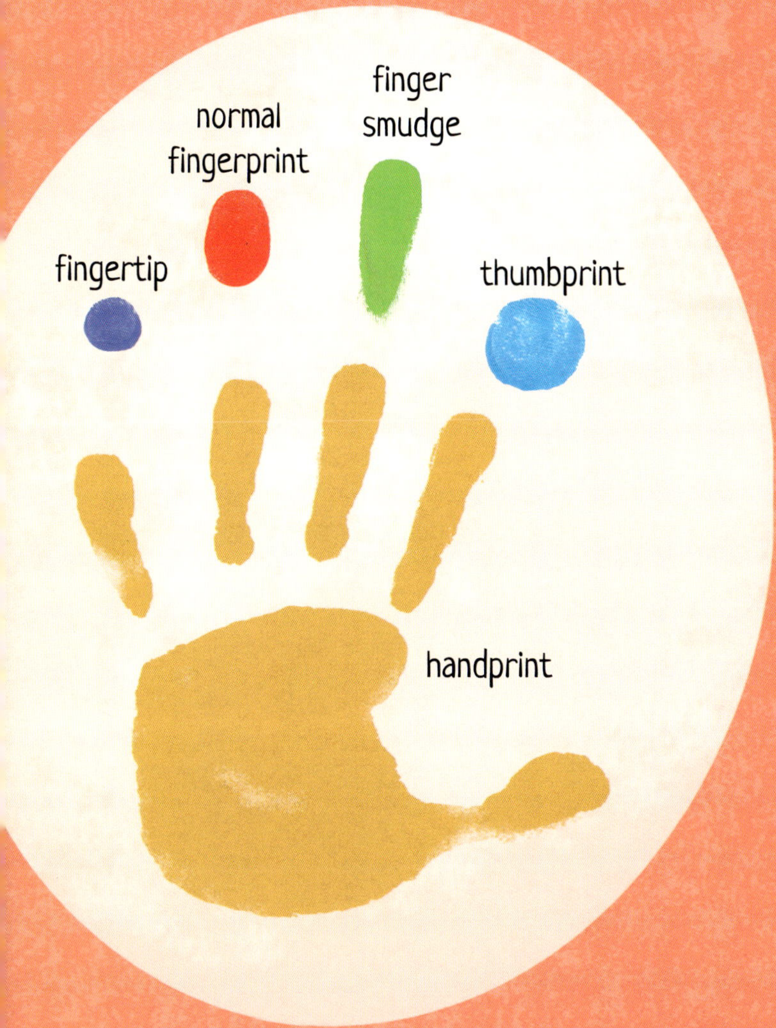

OUR TOP TIPS:

1. Make sure you have a wet cloth or tissues nearby to change the paint on your fingers.
2. Only add a tiny amount of water to your paints, or they'll become too runny.
3. Experiment with how much paint you put on your finger. The smaller the amount of paint, the quicker the print will dry!
4. Leave your prints to dry before you add the black line work.
5. You may find it easier to make some prints by turning the page around or upside down.

WISE OWL

Follow these steps to make an adorable owl.

FRIENDLY FOX

Use different shades of orange to make this cheerful creature.

1

2

3

4

5

FANTASTIC FLAMINGO

Have your pink paints at the ready to make this eye-catching bird!

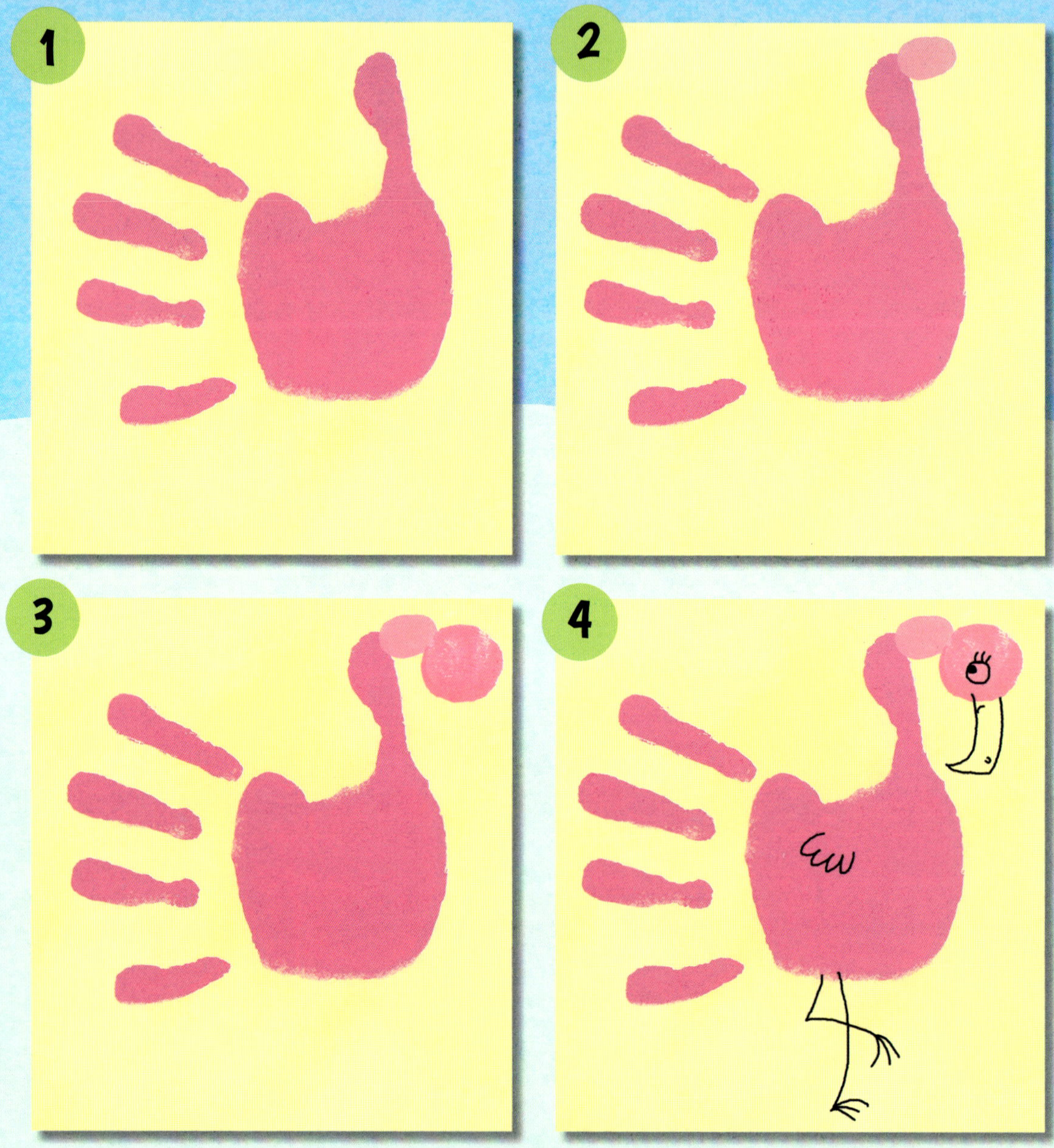

GRIZZLY BEAR

Follow the steps to make a bear on the prowl ...

... or paint a bear stopping to rest.

SPOTTED LEOPARD

Add spots to your handprint to make this big cat.

PLAYFUL MONKEY

Here's how to make a swinging monkey.

Now, make a baby monkey!

POSING PEACOCK

Use your handprint to make a bird with eye-catching feathers.

1

2

3

4

HAPPY CATERPILLAR

Can you create a crawling caterpillar?

1

2

3

4

Add some extra legs to turn it into a millipede!

5

SLOW AND STEADY

Follow the steps to make a really cute tortoise.

1

2

3

4

5

STRIPY ZEBRA

Can you create a zebra using your handprint?

JUNGLE FLOCK

Here's how to paint a perching parrot.

And here's a flying parrot! Can you make one, too?

LiTTLE LiZARD

Can you make a scampering lizard?

1

2

3

4

BUZZiNG BEE

Here's how to make a smiling bee.

FLYING FRIENDS

Will you make a beautiful butterfly ...

... or a magnificent moth?

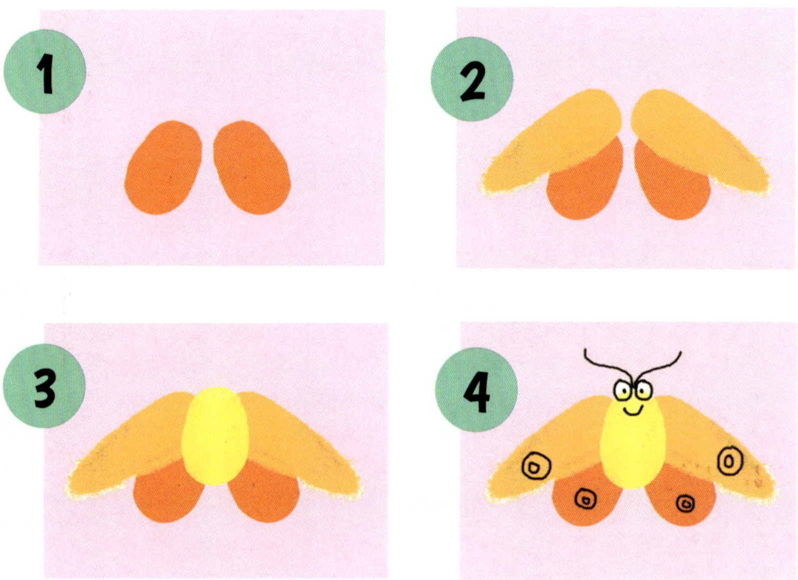

SNAPPING CROC

Here's how to paint a hungry crocodile.

AWESOME OSTRICH

Use your whole hand to create this huge bird.

HAPPY HiPPO

Follow the steps to make a cheerful hippo.

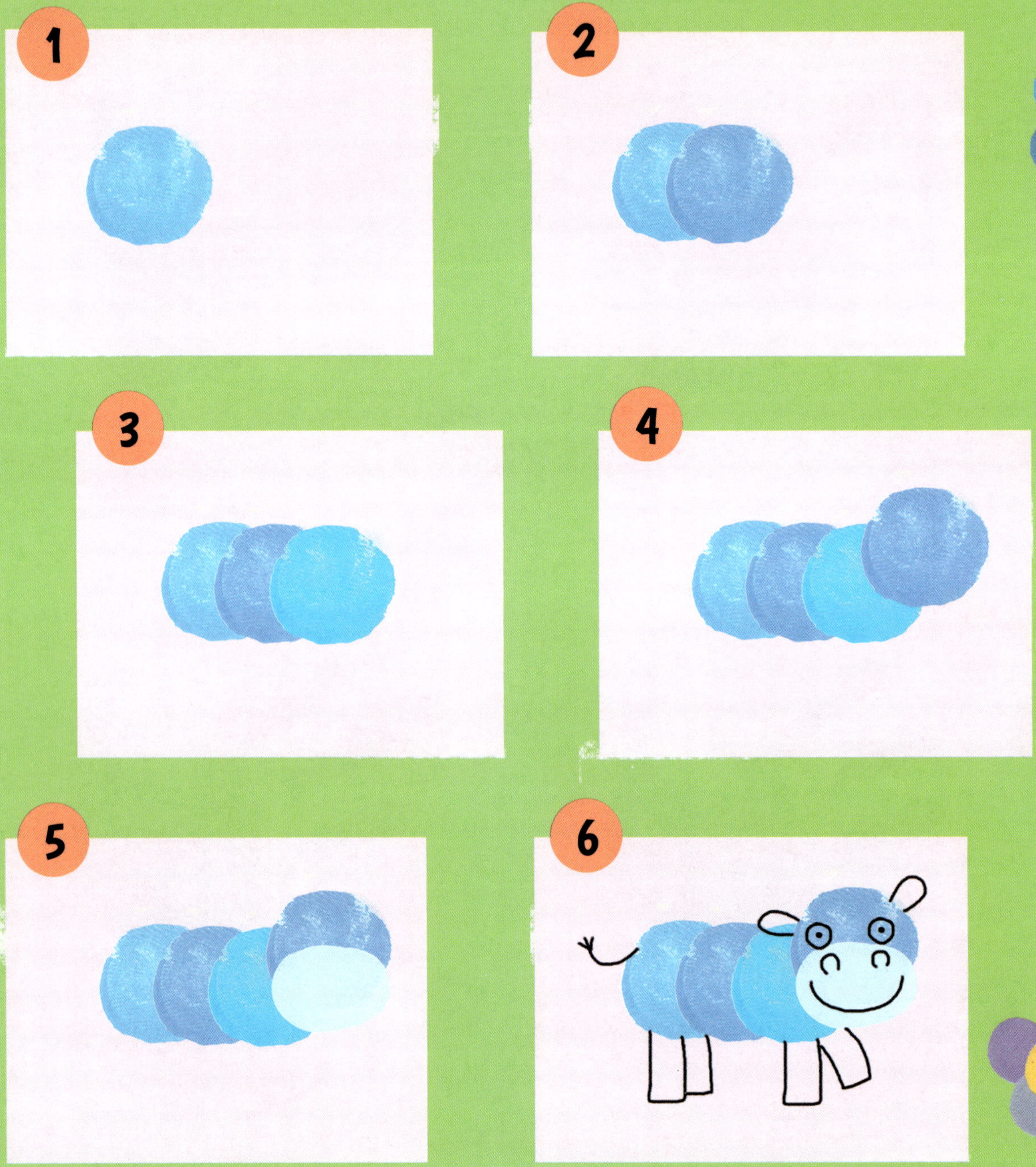

JUNGLE TiGER

Roar! Use fingerprints to paint this fierce animal.

1

2

3

4

POND LiFE

Follow the steps to make a swimming tadpole.

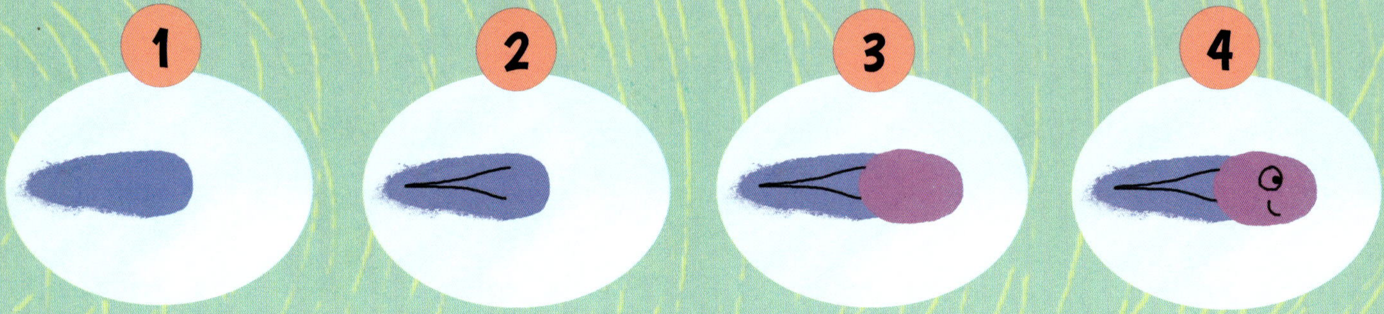

Tadpoles turn into frogs! Can you make the frog below?

BUSY BEAVER

Here's how to make a cute face.

Now, make a beaver's body!

MIGHTY ELEPHANT

Use your handprint to make this mighty creature.

SLITHERING SNAKE

Here's how to make this coiled reptile.

SPINNING SPIDER

Follow the steps to create this eight-legged creature.

1

2

3

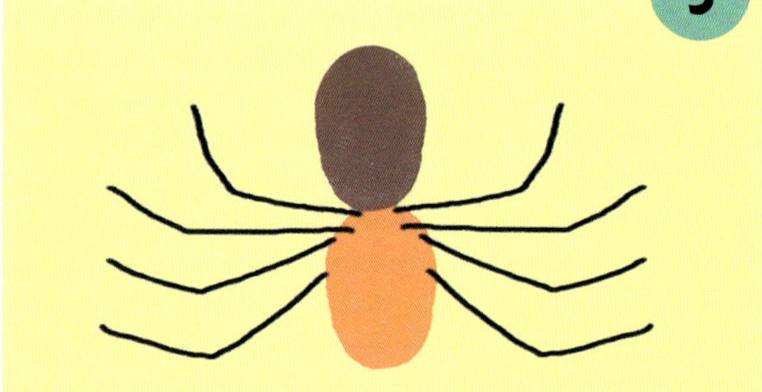

4

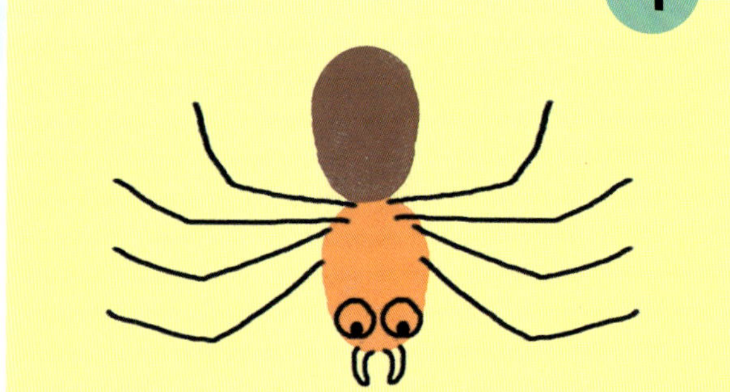

CUTE PANDA

Try painting a panda face.

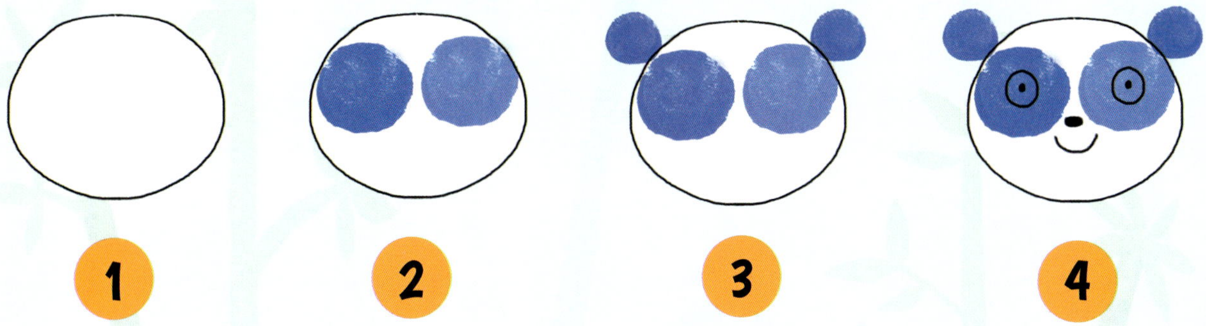

Or try painting a whole panda body!

TOUGH RHiNO

Follow the steps to create this horned animal.

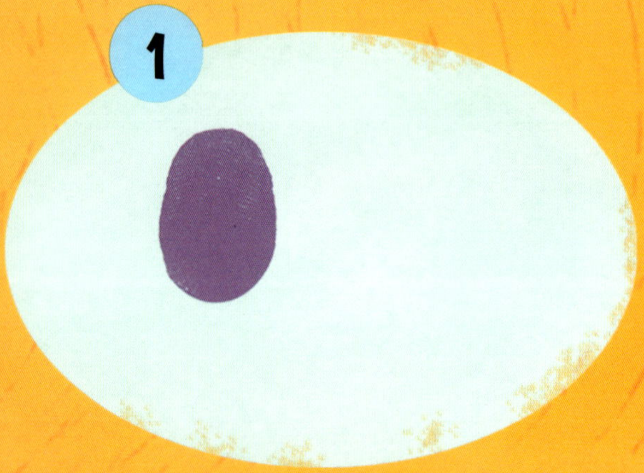

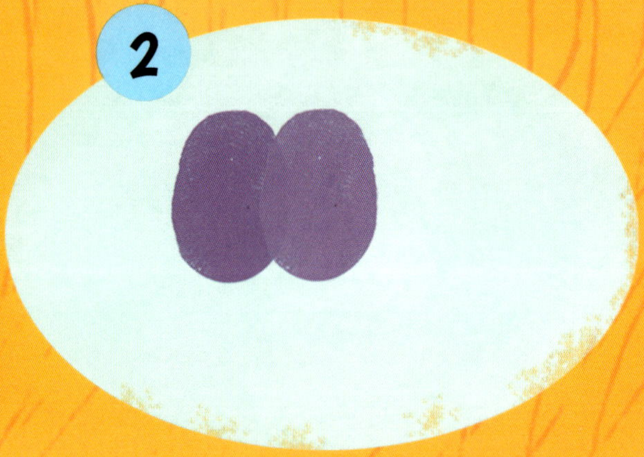

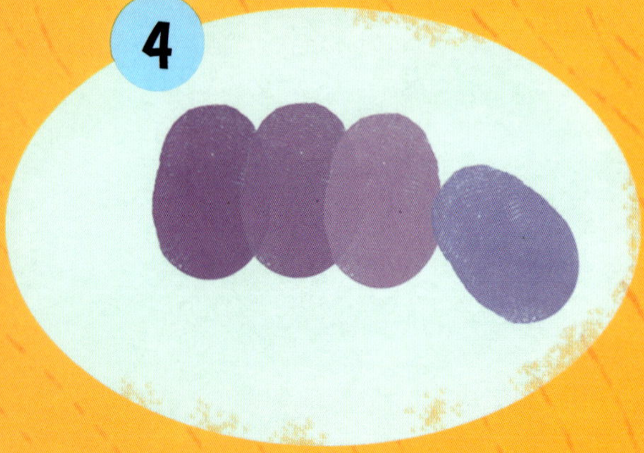

JUMPiNG ANTELOPE

Can you paint this leaping animal?

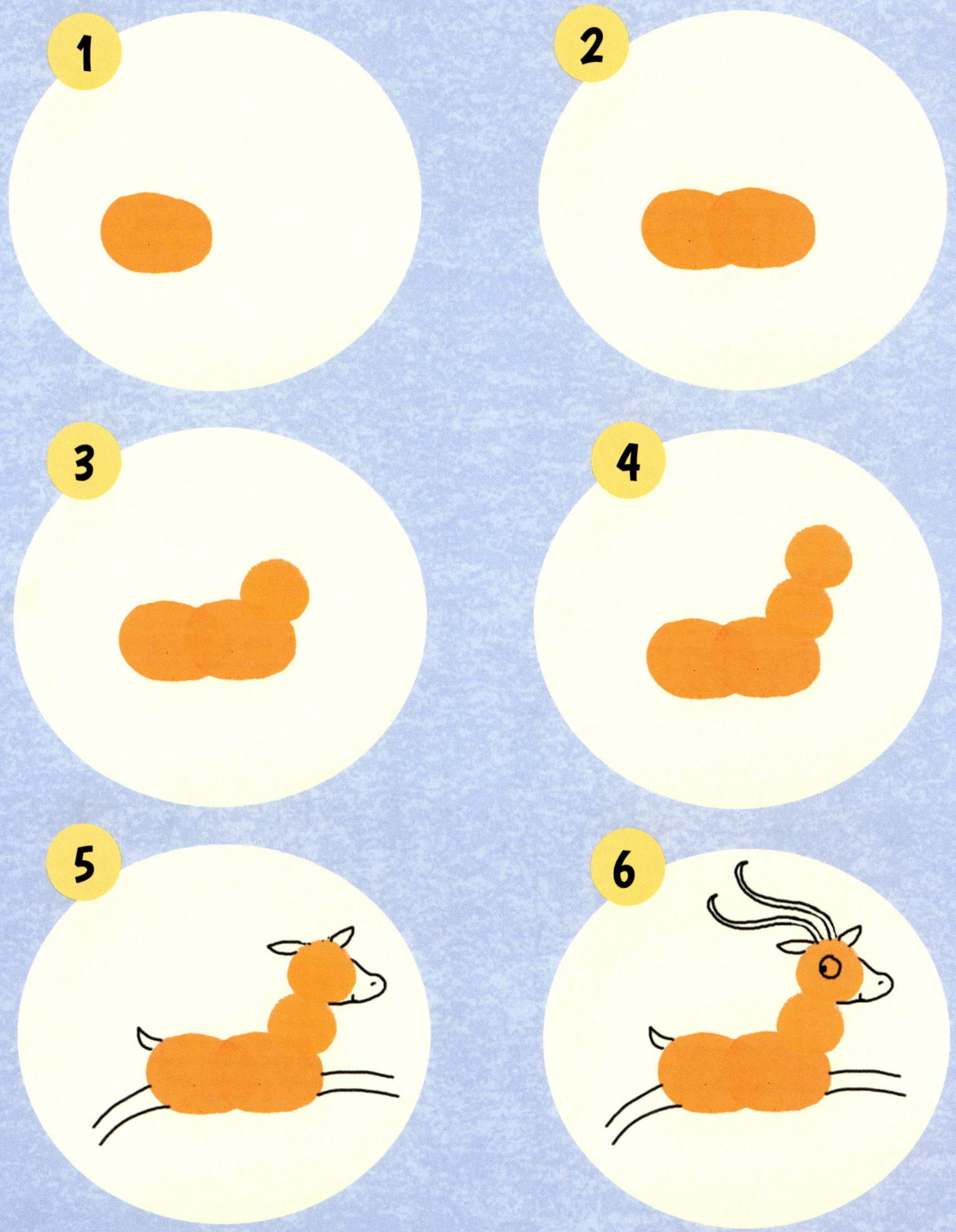

PRANCING REINDEER

Use your whole hand to make this wintry animal.

RED ROBiN

Now let's make a little red robin!

1

2

3

4

FURTHER INFORMATION

Books

Balart, Maite. *Fingerprint & Draw: Animals & Insects*. Lake Forest, CA: Walter Foster Jr., 2017.

Deuchars, Marion. *Let's Make Some Great Fingerprint Art*. London, England: Laurence King Publishing, 2012.

Nuytten, Bobbie. *Fingerprint Animals*. North Mankato, MN: Picture Window Books, 2016.

Websites

For web resources related to the subject of this book, go to: www.windmillbooks.com/weblinks and select this book's title.

INDEX